Around the World in 72 Days

T0337363

Contents

Written by Liz Miles

Illustrated by Monica Auriemma
and Martin Sanders

Collins

Nellie Bly's challenge

Nellie Bly was born in the United States of America in 1864. She became a reporter.

In Nellie's time, travel was tricky and slow.

Nellie read a story in which a man travelled around the world in eighty days.

She challenged herself to complete this trip in
seventy days, in a real-life adventure.

Departure

Nellie's boss said she needed a chaperone (a person joining her to keep her safe), but Nellie went alone. She just took a little lightweight satchel.

6

Nellie's departure was at 9:40 a.m.
on 14 November 1889.

The adventure began on a steamship.
There were no planes.

Nellie was unlucky on her departure. She got seasick!

People wondered whether Nellie would be up to the challenge. Would she survive disease, fever and storms?

Speed

To beat the eighty-day challenge, Nellie had to catch ships and trains on time.

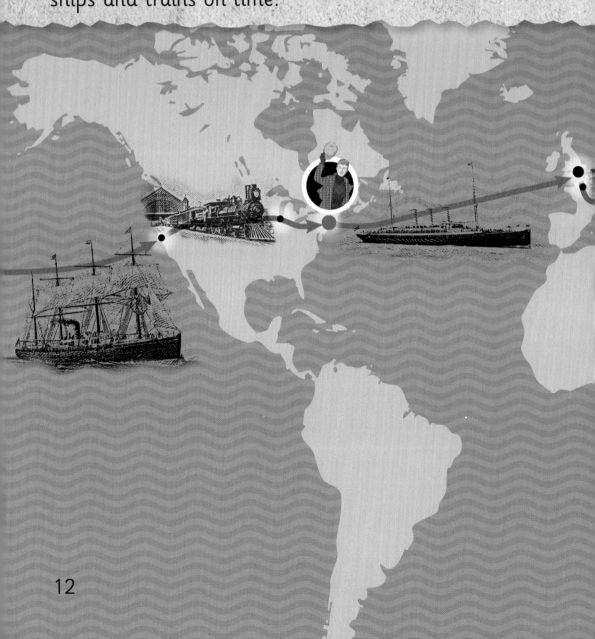

Nellie raged when a ship's departure was late.

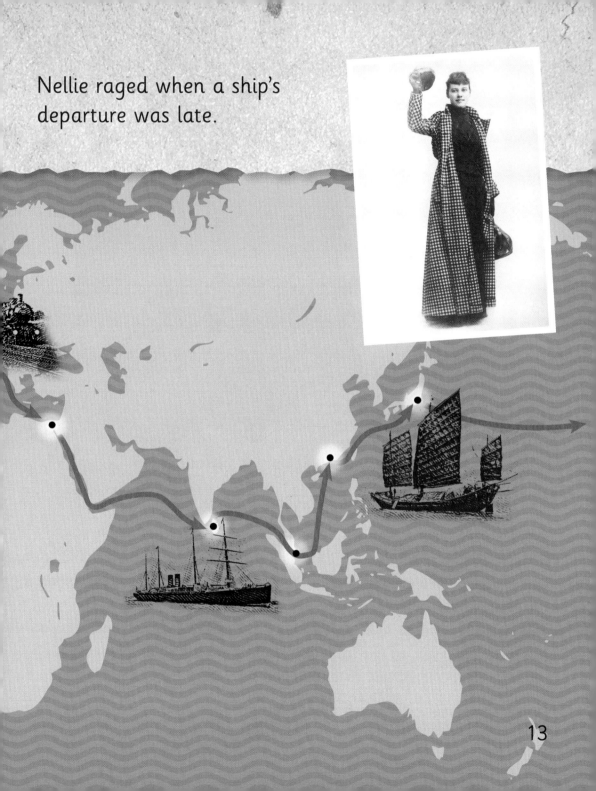

While waiting for ships, she reported on nature and festive events.

She battled with rainy days and even storms.

Nellie was pleased when she got midway round the world and reached Hong Kong. She was 2 days ahead at this stage!

But then she was unlucky. Her ship to Japan was five days late.

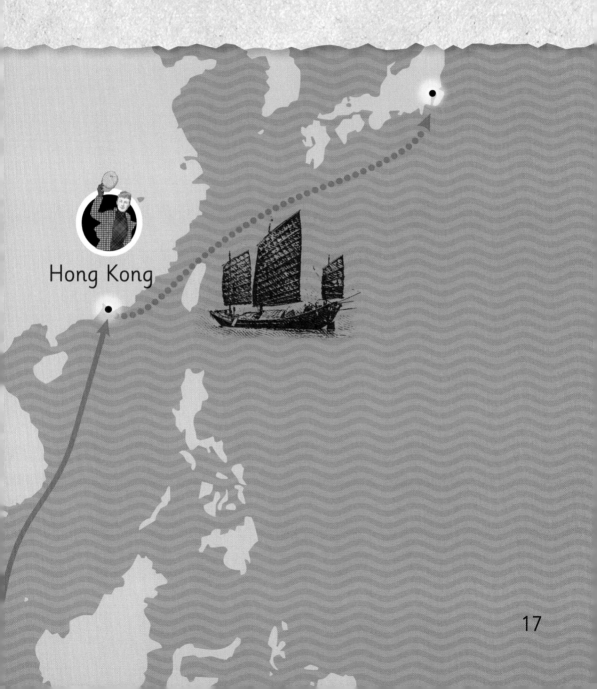

Hong Kong

On 7 January, Nellie had just twenty-five days to battle across eight thousand miles of sea.

When she arrived on land, there was a severe snowstorm. This meant Nellie had to catch a different train to complete her journey.

Triumphant

Nellie completed the adventure in 72 days, setting a world record for travelling around the globe.

She put the key stages of her adventure in a book.
Her story still inspires people today.

Nellie's journey

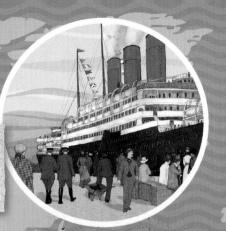

Day 1:
14 November 1889,
United States

Day 72:
25 January 1890,
United States

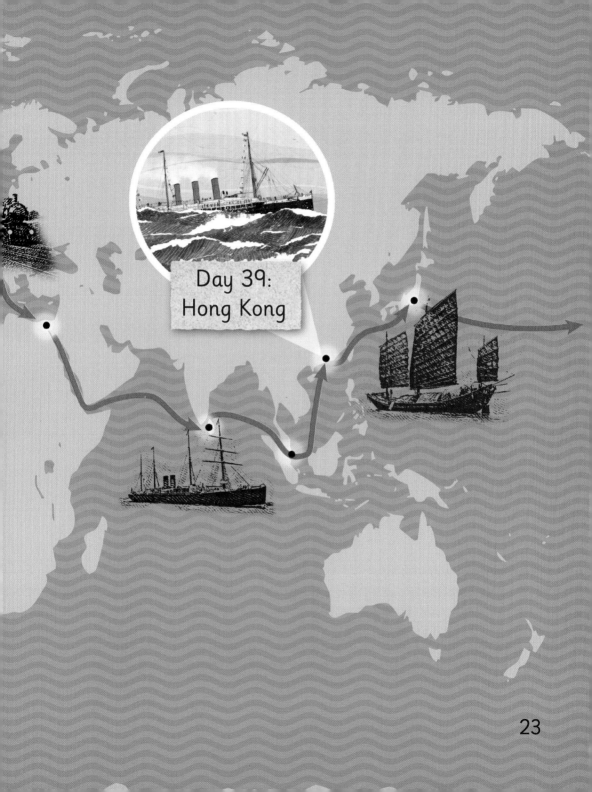

Day 39:
Hong Kong

After reading

Letters and Sounds: Phase 5

Word count: 300

Focus phonemes: /ai/ a, eigh /j/ g, ge /ch/ tch, t /ee/ e, y, ey, e-e /w/ wh /igh/ y /l/ le /f/ ph /v/ ve /z/ se /oo/ u /sh/ ch

Common exception words: of, to, the, said, were, people, today

Curriculum links: Geography: geographical skills and fieldwork; History: significant individuals

National Curriculum learning objectives: Reading/word reading: read accurately by blending sounds in unfamiliar words containing GPCs that have been taught; Reading/comprehension: discussing word meanings, linking new meanings to those already known

Developing fluency

- Your child may enjoy hearing you read the book.
- You could try taking turns to read a page. Model reading with lots of expression and encourage your child to do the same.

Phonic practice

- Help your child to get quicker at reading multi-syllable words. Look at the following words: exactly   slippery   adventure
- Ask your child to:
  - Sound talk and blend each syllable "chunk".
  - Then read each chunk in turn.
  - Now read the whole word quickly.

Extending vocabulary

- On page 3, travel is described as **tricky** and **slow**. Ask your child if they can think of other words the author could have used to describe what travel was like for Nellie. (e.g. *difficult, boring*)
- On page 13, it says that Nellie **raged** when a ship was late leaving. Ask your child if they can think of other words the author could have used to describe how Nellie felt. (e.g. *was angry, fumed, exploded*)
- On page 19, it says that the snowstorm was **severe**. Ask your child if they can think of other words the author could have used to describe the snowstorm. (e.g. *bad, heavy*)